Every Now & Then

Photographs

by

Michael J. Shaw & Frank M. Sutcliffe

A fascinating comparison between digital imaging in the 21st Century and glass plate photography of Victorian times.

This collection of sixty photographs allows us to view two periods in the history of a small coastal town separated by 120 years.

Dedication:
For my wife Tricia,
who made this dream come true!

The Sutcliffe Gallery
1 Flowergate
Whitby
YO21 3BA
01947 602239
www.sutcliffe-gallery.co.uk

Michael J. Shaw

Frank M. Sutcliffe

First Published 2002

Published and © 2002 by:

The Sutcliffe Gallery,
1 Flowergate, Whitby, North Yorkshire,
YO21 3BA, England. Tel: 01947 602239

by agreement with Whitby Literary & Philosophical Society

Special Thanks to:

Bill Eglon Shaw (my father) for his help and encouragement.

All the people who had the patience to pose for me in the 'Now' photographs.

ISBN Numbers:

Soft Cover: 0 9541860 0 1

Hard Cover: 0 9541860 1 X

INTRODUCTION

This book has taken many years to materialise into something more than one of my dreams...for too long it had been just one of those 'good ideas' that I had not found time to do anything about. In the past, one or two abortive attempts to start a 'before and after' collection of photographs had ground to a halt, partly due to me thinking that the project was just too ambitious to succeed.

The advent of digital photography has spurred me on to produce this selection of modern images of Whitby which people can contrast and compare with Frank Meadow Sutcliffe's Whitby 120 years ago. I would like to take this opportunity to state emphatically that I have never ever hoped to match the artistry and quality of work produced by Frank Sutcliffe, but thought that a pictorial comparison of life in the 1880s with the 21st century would produce an interesting book of photographs.

As much as I have really enjoyed producing this book, to a certain extent I have been a little constrained by having to take my photographs from the same (or similar) viewpoint and camera angle as Sutcliffe, which sometimes made me conscious that I was just 'copying' his work. To hopefully relieve this copycat syndrome, I have included in the book one or two of my own photographs which still have a similar 'feel' to that of Sutcliffe's, but also have their own individuality.

In Victorian times, Whitby was often described as a 'Photographer's Mecca', mainly due to many people throughout the country having seen exhibitions of the superb work of Frank Meadow Sutcliffe. The portrayal of the town in such an artistic light enticed other photographers to visit Whitby and attempt to produce similar results!

Whitby still has a great wealth of character (and characters!) to appeal to the modern photographer which many other towns have lost. Consequently this has led to a number of the 'now' photographs in this book having a similar appearance to the 'then' Sutcliffe images.

Frank Meadow Sutcliffe was born in Headingley, Leeds in 1853, the son of Thomas Sutcliffe a watercolour artist whose enthusiasm and encouragement helped Frank in his pursuit of photography. In 1871 Frank's father died, the same year that the Sutcliffe family moved to Whitby. In 1875 after an abortive effort to set up a photographic business in Tunbridge Wells, Sutcliffe returned to Whitby and turned a disused jet workshop in Waterloo Yard into a studio.
Sutcliffe made his living from taking portraits in this studio, but his real passion was capturing Whitby and its people with a rare flair and talent for which he was awarded sixty-two gold, silver and bronze medals from exhibitions around the world.

In 1922 Frank Sutcliffe retired from photography and sold his business along with the collection of over 1600 award winning glass plate negatives.
Sutcliffe's retirement lasted for at least one week after which he became the curator of Whitby museum, a position he held up to his death in 1941.

In 1935 The Royal Photographic Society conferred on Sutcliffe their Honorary Fellowship, the highest distinction which can be awarded in the photographic world.

In 1959 my father Bill Eglon Shaw, himself a professional photographer, bought the collection of Sutcliffe negatives along with the studio at 1 Flowergate which is now The Sutcliffe Gallery where we publish postcards, greeting cards, reproduction prints, photographs and books illustrating the superb work of Frank Meadow Sutcliffe.

This book sees a departure from our previous publications with the introduction of colour photography which was deemed necessary to create a true contrast between 'Now and Then'. Monochrome photography is often considered to have more feeling and artistry than colour work, and the comparisons in this book will no doubt confirm this, yet it is still intriguing to see how very little a remote fishing town in North Yorkshire has changed in 120 years.

'Every Now & Then' hopefully illustrates that the passing of time has not significantly changed the essence of Whitby, one of Britain's most beautiful and pictorial towns.

The back cover illustrates the two types of camera used to take the photographs in this book. On the right is a modern digital SLR, an Olympus E10 and on the left a whole plate camera which holds glass negatives 6.5" x 8.5" in size.

Three of the 'modern' photographs in this book have been taken with a Nikon 401s film camera in the mid 1990s, namely; 'Endeavour Returns, 1997' (page 16), 'View from the Railway Station' (page 34) and 'Abbey in the Mist' (page42).

"Wings above the Water"

Taken on a bright summer's afternoon on New Quay Road, Whitby, this photograph shows a backdrop of newer houses and flats built in the 1960s.
St Michael's Church and School were demolished in the late 1950s and were both quite a landmark along Church Street. Railings have been added for safety along the quayside within the last few years. The boat on the left is Berwick registered with its modern radar equipment clearly visible.

"Boats Moored at the New Quay"

The 'Welfare', a Hartlepool registered lugger, seen here drying her nets. This had to be done frequently as they were all made from natural fibres. Although they were also regularly 'barked' in a brew made from oak bark, which gave the nets their distinctive colour, they were prone to rot very quickly if stowed away wet.

Ref. 17-26

"Above Tate Hill Beach, 2001"

A solitary fishing boat glides towards the harbour mouth.

At first glance, very little seems to have altered in this photograph in comparison with that taken by Sutcliffe in the 1880s..... then you may notice the absence of the windmill (Union Mill) and the addition of the Metropole Towers, also St. Hilda's church which was built in 1885.

"Above Tate Hill Beach, circa 1880"
Whitby from St. Mary's parish church overlooking Tate hill beach with the west cliff in the background, the Royal Hotel being the dominant building in the centre.
A much greater number of fishing boats can be seen in this photograph compared to the modern scene, an indication of the sad state of the fishing industry today.

Ref: 13-35

"Church Street, 2001"
Although the buildings in the background have altered very little, this modern photograph more than any other shows how much Whitby has changed in character. Taken around the end of July 2001, this view gives a good indication of what Whitby is about.....tourism!
In the last few years Church Street has become *the* street for holiday makers, offering lots of interesting galleries, bookshops, craft shops and cafes.

"Church Street, circa 1880"
Known as Kirkgate in the 14th century, this is the oldest part of the town.
Church Street leads from the foot of the 199 steps, the pathway to St. Mary's Parish Church, to Spital Bridge and the Whitehall Ship Yard in the upper harbour.
The carefully chosen lighting does much to enhance this everyday record of a Victorian street.

Ref: 3-52

"On the Capstan, 2001"
Taken on the East Pier, Jack looks down on his father, Ed Mann from the top of the capstan.
This pier is now accessible, following temporary closure for work being carried out after serious cliff erosion.

"On the Capstan, circa 1880"
 Two fishermen each smoking a clay pipe on one of the piers.
The wooden capstan was used to haul in be-calmed vessels which were too large to be towed up the harbour.

Ref: 12-13

"Misty Morning, 2001"
Taken one misty September morning at 8.00a.m. from the east side of Whitby's swing bridge, looking up the River Esk.
The back of Grape Lane can be seen on the left. Compared with Sutcliffe's photograph this view of Church Street is much more open.
This is due to the post World War II demolition of Harker's jet works together with St. Michael's Church and school.

"Misty Morning, circa 1880"
Old Church Street from the corner of Whitby bridge. Harker's Jet workshops with the large windows, above a coal depot, occupy the site of the present slipway. In the background are St. Michael's Church and School, together with the Board School.
A paddle steamer tug can be seen as well as several small laid-up sailing vessels.

Ref: C10

"St. Hilda's Abbey, 2001"

Taken February 2001, this image was one of the first to be photographed with the 'Now and Then' project specifically in mind. The Abbey and pond have changed little in over 120 years.

These ancient ruins of the Abbey dominate the East Cliff and have long been used as a landmark by seamen approaching Whitby harbour.

"St. Hilda's Abbey, circa 1880"
This has been a religious site since 656 A.D. when King Oswy of Northumberland founded St. Hilda's Saxon monastery.
The early building was destroyed by Vikings and was refounded in 1077.
Caedmon, the first English poet lived and worked here as a cow-herd. Perhaps this thought did not escape Sutcliffe as he was taking this photograph.

Ref: 4-3

"Endeavour Returns"
HM Bark Endeavour entering the harbour mouth on Friday 9th May 1997, one of the most memorable days in Whitby's history. The number of people who flocked to the town to welcome the replica of the Endeavour was simply staggering, probably never to be repeated even when she returns again in June, 2002. The replica of Captain Cook's famous ship was built in Fremantle, Western Australia and is commanded by Captain Chris Blake.

"Rachel Lotinga"

The 'Rachel Lotinga', a variant of the brig-rigged sailing ship known as a 'snow', aground on Whitby's harbour bar.
With a displacement of 242 tons, she was built in Sunderland in 1855 and registered at Whitby in October 1874.

Ref: 10-45

"Fish Auction, 2001"

An early morning insight into a Whitby fish market, now under cover and protected from the elements these buildings are insulated and chilled. Plastic fish boxes, more hygienic and easily stacked, are now used instead of wooden barrels.

'Alliance Fish', established around 1989, are the main dealers in the Scarborough and Whitby area. David Winspear, the managing director, can be seen on the far right of the photograph, wearing white trousers.

"Fish Market, circa 1880"
Whitby Fish Market at 'Coffee House End'. Men who have been identified, working from the left are; with book and wearing white round-crowned hat, Edward Turner, a fish merchant; next to him in peaked cap, Joseph Blackburn of Kiln Yard; with bowler hat and hands on hips, Christopher 'Kit' Eglon, fish auctioneer of Elephant and Castle Yard, Haggersgate (great, great Grandfather of Michael Shaw); next to him, pipe in mouth, 'Bill Tom' Winspear; in uniform, Naval Reservist 'Jolka' Eglon of The Cragg; the two men at right are Robert Coulson and Robert Hansell, fishermen, both of whom were later drowned at sea.

Ref: B28

"Captain Cook's View"
The statue of Captain Cook overlooks Whitby from this viewpoint.
Erosion of the East Cliff has caused quite a number of buildings to fall into the sea since Sutcliffe's day. The bandstand in the centre of this photograph was built in the year 2000.
A TV booster mast is a rather jarring intrusion on the landscape, satellite transmissions may one day allow it to be removed!

"East Cliff and Tate Hill Sands"
A clear view of Whitby's East Cliff and Tate Hill sands where washing can be seen laid out to dry on the beach.
In the foreground several 'bathing machines' can be seen. These were wheeled huts which were drawn down to the water's edge by horses allowing bathers to step modestly into the sea.

Ref: 13-38

"Looking Fetching on the Lines!"
Paula Visker (nee Barker), a direct descendant of Lizzie Alice Hawksfield, stands outside her place of work in Flowergate.
Manager of the Scarborough Building Society in Whitby, Paula aged 24, was married in the summer of 2001.

"Fetching in the Lines"
The fishergirl holding the 'long line' is Lizzie Alice Hawksfield.
The girls and fishermens' wives collected the mussels which were used as bait, often walking up to six miles each way to do so.
'Mucking' (cleaning the lines and hooks of old bait and other debris), 'skaning' (removing the mussels from their shells) and baiting a 'long line' earned them 9d.

Ref: D49

"Bridge from the Fish Quay"
An atmospheric view from the fish quay looking along Marine Parade and St. Ann's Staith towards Whitby's swing bridge. This bridge was built in 1909 and still opens daily to allow larger vessels in and out of the upper harbour.
The sky in this photograph is uncannily similar in appearance to the one taken by Frank Meadow Sutcliffe in the late 1880s.

"Steam Tug in Lower Harbour"
A twin-paddle steam tug 'The Flying Spray', from the Clyde is moored at Coffee House Corner in Whitby's lower harbour. Taken circa 1895.
The block of buildings in the centre background were demolished in the early 1970s.
The bridge in this photograph was built in 1835 at a cost of £10,000 and replaced in 1909.

Ref: B33

"Market Day, 2001"
In 2001 a market was held on a Tuesday and Saturday, the latter being the more popular.
This photograph is taken from the upper window of what was 'Burberry's' clothing factory, which closed in August 1998.
The covered stalls are selling the wares of today, mobile phone covers and soft toys replacing the vegetables and cheeses of the Victorian market stall.

"Market Place, Whitby, 1884"

Whitby Market Place, Church Street, in 1884 with the Old Town Hall in the background.

In the 17th century, the Market was moved to its present site, depicted in this photograph, from the bottom of Golden Lion Bank. This was due to increased traffic to the East side via a wooden drawbridge built by Sir Hugh Cholmley.

In 1884, the rents for the market stalls ranged from 1s. 6d to 2s. 0d. per day.

Ref: 12-11

"Peter N. Thompson, M.B.E."
Member of Whitby Lifeboat from 1966 - 1993 and coxswain from 1977 - 1993.
After Henry Freeman, Peter is the longest serving Whitby coxswain. He was awarded the M.B.E. in 1993 for service to the R.N.L.I.
The other medal Peter is wearing is a 'Bronze' awarded in 1988 for gallantry whilst rescuing the yacht 'Cymba', just off the East Pier at Whitby.

"Henry Freeman"
Sole survivor of the Whitby Lifeboat disaster of 1861, Henry Freeman was a lifeboatman for over forty years. The twelve other members of the crew were drowned when this tragedy occurred close by Whitby's West Pier. His survival was attributed to the wearing of a recently introduced Board of Trade cork life jacket which the rest of the crew would not wear due to its restricting and uncomfortable design when rowing the lifeboat.

Ref: 6-89

"The Fish Pier, Whitby 2001"
The Lifeboat launch stands beside the old fish pier on Whitby's east side.
St. Mary's parish church crowns the green cliff, with the attractive cottages and houses nestling beneath.
The original fish pier has been clad with a timber extension to increase its area.

Taken with a Nikon 880 digital compact camera.

"The Fish Pier, Whitby, circa 1880"
The Fish Pier in the 1880s with washing hanging out to dry below the smoky rooftops.
The haze in the background was a common feature in Victorian Whitby due to most people having open fires. The chimney smoke mixing with the fog helped to create Sutcliffe's trademark of atmospheric backdrops to his harbour scenes.

Ref: C17

"Gameboy"
This happy band of children pose together in similar formation to those in 'Jacks'.
Note the 'Gameboy' computer game on the girls lap and the aluminium scooters so popular with the youngsters of today.
The children are from left to right; Joe Hudson, Verity Clawson, Samuel Whitfield-Waring, Faye Whitfield, Sophie Whitfield and Jessica Bennett.

"Jacks"

Children playing what is known locally as 'Jacks', a game played with a round stone or small ball and five stones. The ball was thrown in the air and the object of the game was to pick up as many stones with one hand before the ball hit the ground.

Taken outside David Storry's grocery shop at the foot of the 199 steps which lead up to St. Mary's Parish Church, Whitby.

Ref: 20-17

"View from the Railway Station"

A view through the railway station doorway showing a huge transporter lorry instead of the three masted ship 'Anna', seen in the photograph taken by Frank Meadow Sutcliffe. The dock has been reduced over the years to make room for roads and car parking. In the background can be seen the Abbey and Abbey house, the latter to be made into a visitor centre for 2002 by English Heritage. (Taken with Nikon 401s film camera circa 1994)

"Through the Station Doorway"
Taken on 19th September 1895, Whitby Dock End in the upper harbour, framed by the entrance to the North Eastern Railway Company's town station. The three masted ship 'Anna', is moored at the quayside. This area has changed considerably since Sutcliffe's time with quite a large section of the harbour having been reclaimed and developed.

Ref: 28-12

35

"Walking the Dogs"
Taken at 5pm on a February afternoon in 2001, this sunlit frosty photograph shows the top of Green Lane looking towards the west side of Whitby.
Green Lane runs between Church Street and the Abbey with its new main entrance and car park created by English Heritage in 2001.
This photograph was taken with a Nikon 880 compact digital camera.

"Pier Road, Whitby"
An almost 'stage set' effect is suggested in this evocative photograph by Frank Meadow Sutcliffe. It depicts Pier Road, Coffee House Corner and Whitby's lower harbour in the 1890s.

Haggersgate may be seen in the background, with the Neptune Inn on the corner, dimly leading off into the distance at the right of the Marine Hotel.

Ref: 11-34

"View from Spion Kop, 2001"

This elevated view of Whitby and the upper harbour has not changed greatly in 120 years, one of the obvious exceptions being the swing bridge.
'Marine Cafe' can be clearly seen on the right of the picture and the red building on the far left, houses the inshore Lifeboat.
Looking towards the horizon, a lot more houses can be seen, which have been built to cope with the increased population since Sutcliffe's day.

"View from Spion Kop, circa 1880"
Sutcliffe has photographed Whitby from this viewpoint on numerous occasions but not often under such clear conditions. Misty and atmospheric scenes of the town are more typical of his work. Taken from an excellent vantage point called 'Spion Kop', also known as 'Burtree Crag'.
The large building on the far left was to become a clothing factory for 'Burberry's' of London in January 1973 until its closure in August 1998.

Ref: 8-26

"Dave Locker"

Now retired, David James Locker spent his working life as a fisherman. He still lives on Sandside, Whitby, the area where he was born on 29th June 1938. On 12th July 1958 he married local lass, Jean Hansell. In the 1960s Dave played for Fishburn Park football team, a local club.

Whitby's two piers can be seen in the background with the East pier extension clearly visible, whilst a stack of lobster pots form an impromptu seat in the sun for Dave.

"Tom Langlands"
Thomas Smith Langlands on Tate Hill Pier, Whitby. Born 1853 at Seahouses, Northumbria, he died in 1923. Joining Whitby Lifeboat crew
aged 18, he was two years later appointed second coxswain at Upgang, a couple of miles along the coast from Whitby.
In 1877, at the age of twenty four, he was made coxswain and was awarded the 'Gold Medal' for his brave rescues from the
Red Cross hospital ship, S. S. Rohilla, which sank off Whitby in October 1914.

Ref: 19-15

"Hazy Sunlight over Whitby Abbey"
The Gothic ruins of Whitby's famous St. Hilda's Abbey are still fascinating in eerie lighting conditions such as these. English Heritage are custodians of these historic remains, and it is one of their most popular sites in the country, due to its imposing position above the town and significance in the history of religion.
(Taken with a Nikon 401s film camera in 1993)

"Whitby Abbey Shrouded in Mist"
This unusual photograph of St. Hilda's Abbey, by Frank Sutcliffe, shows the East transept and impressive East window with fallen masonry in the foreground. The sea mist, which veils the Abbey and gives this photograph a mysterious ghostly feel, can cover the town very rapidly and alter the landscape dramatically.

Ref: 6-94

"Victorian Jet Works"

This Jet works was originally in Burns Yard, Whitby, registered in 1867. In the early 1990s, David (Gussie) Freeman moved the fully preserved tools and machinery, to its present site at the end of cobbled Church street, near the 199 steps to St. Hilda's Abbey.

Hal Redvers-Jones, seen here in the photograph, has run this jet works since he took it over in the mid 1990s.

"Jet Workers, Whitby"
During the latter half of the 19th century the manufacture of jewellery from locally mined jet was one of Whitby's main industries. Situated in Haggersgate and owned by William Wright, this was the only jet workshop equipped with gas-engine powered lathes.
Taken by Frank Meadow Sutcliffe in 1890.

Ref: 27-38

"Colin Doran"

A familiar character around Whitby. Colin is a keen cyclist, photographer and amateur artist, and a nephew of the Doran brothers who were well known local photographers until the 1970s.

Dorans Photographers was founded in 1902 by William Eakins Doran, grandfather of Colin.

" 'Tarry' Wilson"
A studio portrait of 'Tarry' Wilson. Sutcliffe's approach to studio work was essentially one of great simplicity, shunning the elaborate settings used by many of his contemporaries.
Although there are not many studio portraits in the collection that made him famous, Frank Meadow Sutcliffe made his living from photographing sitters from all over the region.

47

Ref: 30-4

"Sunlight on Cowbar Nab, Staithes"

Three children and their father play on the beach at Staithes, October 2001.

Cowbar Nab is spotlit by the sun forming a strong focal point of the photograph.

The Lifeboat house can be seen in the background with large red doors and R.N.L.I. flag flying.

A group of fishermen congregate outside the 'Cod & Lobster' inn, which is very different in size and shape to the building of the same name in the Sutcliffe photograph.

"Cowbar Nab, Staithes"

Many of Sutcliffe's photographs were taken at Staithes, about nine miles north west along the coast from Whitby. In the late 1800s, practically the whole of the community relied on the fishing industry for its livelihood and around this time forty-two cobles and fourteen larger 'smacks' fished out of Staithes.

The building behind the policeman is the 'Cod and Lobster' inn which was washed away in high seas. The more recent hostelry being much better protected from the waves.

Ref: 9-47

"Digging for Bait at Runswick"
Four people dig for 'lug' worms on Runswick beach with the Lifeboat slipway to their left.
One of the most famous views and most often painted areas of this beautiful coastal village.
The cottage on the right is the only thatched building in the bay and is owned by the sister of the Marquis of Normanby.
In 1901, with most of the men out fishing, an unexpected and violent storm broke and with only a scratch crew to man the Lifeboat, the
women of Runswick courageously dragged the boat down the slipway and launched it into the raging sea, saving the lives of their menfolk.

"Runswick Bay"
Runswick Village and Bay was frequented by the 'Staithes Group' of artists, including Dame Laura Knight, who were inspired by the rugged but picturesque landscape of this area. A painter can be seen on the beach sheltering from the sun under a parasol with his dog by his side.
This peaceful scene taken from the South side of the Bay shows a very calm sea on which three cobles are moored with a fourth one resting on the Lifeboat slipway.

Ref: 8-29

"Fortune's Kippers"

Two ladies near the doorway of this long established smoke-house. One of the women has just bought some of the kippers which are still oak smoked for days to give that original distinctive flavour. Whitby is rightly famous for its kippers produced by Barry and Derek Brown on Henrietta street who continue a long family tradition in smoking herring.

These ladies have a different style of dress from those in Sutcliffe's day, but are probably still discussing 'the price of fish'!

52

"Women in New Way Ghaut"
Taken by Frank Meadow Sutcliffe during the 1890s in one of the many narrow passages leading down to the harbourside.
The edge lighting entering the photograph from the left transforms this from what would have been a rather ordinary figure study to an
arresting picture.

Ref: E4

"Bay Bank, Robin Hoods Bay, 2001"
This very steep bank at Robin Hoods Bay is still quite recognisable, with so many buildings remaining unchanged in structure.
As tourism has grown, many of the houses are now trading as gift shops or galleries.
Wendy Bulmer can be seen leading her horse 'Mac', up the steep hill.

"Bay Bank, Robin Hoods Bay, circa 1880"
This photograph shows what a problem it must have been for pedestrians or a horse and cart to climb the steep incline of Bay Bank when it was wet and muddy!
One of Frank Meadow Sutcliffe's better known photographs of Robin Hoods Bay.

Ref: C12

"Low Row, Sandsend, 2001"

Low Row cottages have changed little externally in over one hundred years, apart from slight modernisation. If the cars and TV aerials were removed from this photograph it would look very similar to the one taken by Sutcliffe, apart from the small wooden bridge over Sandsend beck.

Taken in the late afternoon sunshine, the lighting imparts an attractive glow to the trees in the background, which have matured greatly since Sutcliffe's day.

"Low Row, Sandsend, circa 1880"
Sandsend is considered by many to be one of the most picturesque villages in Britain, where the green countryside literally meets the golden coast.
In Sutcliffe's day all the houses would most certainly have been permanent homes, whereas now, a number of holiday cottages combine with the thriving local community.

Ref: 9-23

"Arguments Yard, 2001"
How very little this yard has changed in over a hundred years, except in improved living conditions.
Local girls Jessica Bennett and Faye Whitfield contentedly soak up the afternoon sunshine.
Jessica sits with her dog 'Ellie', while Faye holds her favourite doll.

"Arguments Yard, Circa 1895"
This yard, like so many in Whitby, was named after a family, in this case the 'Arguments'.
Tourists love having their photograph taken standing beside the sign to this yard!
Quite a number of yards in the town have been demolished over the years to make way for more modern housing, but luckily a few have still survived.
Ref: 4-43

"Beggar's Bridge, 2001"
Beggar's Bridge with Arncliffe woods in the background.
'Fennel' the Border terrier, looks into the River Esk from the lovely stone bridge while the photographer's wife, Tricia sits and reads her book on a bright October day.
The railway bridge in the background, built nearly three hundred years after Beggar's Bridge, carries the Whitby to Middlesbrough trains.

"Lady on Beggar's Bridge"

The legend of the beautiful Beggar's Bridge recounts that Tom Ferris, a poor boy and son of an Egton farmer was courting Agnes Richardson, much to the disapproval of her father the Squire of Glaisdale. Tom decided to go to sea and enlisted on a ship leaving Whitby to join the fleet which was to confront the Armada. The night before the vessel sailed he went to Glaisdale to say goodbye to Agnes. He found the Esk in flood and as there was no bridge spanning the river had to leave without seeing her. He was so disappointed, he made a vow that one day he would build a bridge over the River Esk. As well as fighting the Spaniards, he did some buccaneering and eventually returned a wealthy man to marry Agnes. He built Beggars Bridge in 1619, twelve years before his death. In his will Tom left the village of Glaisdale £8 13s 4d per annum for the upkeep of the church and maintenance of the bridge. This was a large amount of money at the time, and even 250 years on was still being paid.

Ref: 17-11

"Feeding Time"
Using a Nikon 880 digital compact camera, this photograph of sheep was taken along The Carrs, a road running between Sleights and Ruswarp.
The afternoon winter sunshine in February 2001 imparts a warm glow to the picture contrasting with the cold misty background.
Yet to come was the dreaded foot and mouth disease a few weeks after this photograph was taken.

"Sheep & Lambs near Ewe Cote Hall"
A pleasingly composed back-lit group of sheep and lambs in a field between Ewe Cote Hall and the coast.
It appears that Frank Sutcliffe may have been commissioned to take this photograph as it is one of a number taken at this location.

Ref: 24-10